W9-CGL-359

NUMBERS 1–20

Know Your Numbers

SCHOOL

Alex Kuskowski

Consulting Editor, Diane Craig, M.A./Reading Specialist

Sandcastle

An Imprint of Abdo Publishing
www.abdopublishing.com

visit us at www.abdopublishing.com

Published by Abdo Publishing, a division of ABDO, PO Box 398166, Minneapolis, Minnesota 55439. Copyright © 2015 by Abdo Consulting Group, Inc. International copyrights reserved in all countries. No part of this book may be reproduced in any form without written permission from the publisher. SandCastle™ is a trademark and logo of Abdo Publishing.

Printed in the United States of America, North Mankato, Minnesota
062014
092014

Editor: Liz Salzmann
Content Developer: Nancy Tuminelly
Cover and Interior Design: Anders Hanson, Mighty Media, Inc.
Photo Credits: Shutterstock

Library of Congress Cataloging-in-Publication Data
Kuskowski, Alex., author.
 Know your numbers. School / Alex Kuskowski.
    pages cm. -- (Numbers 1-20)
 ISBN 978-1-62403-267-7
1. Counting--Juvenile literature. 2. Cardinal numbers--Juvenile literature. 3. Schools--Juvenile literature. I. Title. II. Title: School.
 QA113.K868 2015
 513.2--dc23
                    2013041910

SandCastle™ Level: Beginning

SandCastle™ books are created by a team of professional educators, reading specialists, and content developers around five essential components—phonemic awareness, phonics, vocabulary, text comprehension, and fluency—to assist young readers as they develop reading skills and strategies and increase their general knowledge. All books are written, reviewed, and leveled for guided reading, early reading intervention, and Accelerated Reader® programs for use in shared, guided, and independent reading and writing activities to support a balanced approach to literacy instruction. The SandCastle™ series has four levels that correspond to early literacy development. The levels are provided to help teachers and parents select appropriate books for young readers.

EMERGING · **BEGINNING** · TRANSITIONAL · FLUENT

Contents

There is 1 school bus.
The bus takes kids to school.

● = 1 = one

1 2 3 4 5 6 7 8 9 10 11 12 13 14 15 16 17 18 19 20

Alyssa and Megan play **violins** in music class. There are 2 violins.

●● = 2 = two

1 2 3 4 5 6 7 8 9 10 11 12 13 14 15 16 17 18 19 20

There are 3 boys going to history class. They walk together.

••• = 3 = three

1 2 **3** 4 5 6 7 8 9 10 11 12 13 14 15 16 17 18 19 20

6

Jessica has 4 schoolbooks.
She takes them to class.

●●●● = 4 = four

1 2 3 **4** 5 6 7 8 9 10 11 12 13 14 15 16 17 18 19 20

Ms. Stein has 5 kids in her class.
They work on math problems.

●●●●● = 5 = five

1 2 3 4 5 6 7 8 9 10 11 12 13 14 15 16 17 18 19 20

There are 6 kids in acting class. They raise their hands to act in a skit.

•••••• = 6 = six

1 2 3 4 5 **6** 7 8 9 10 11 12 13 14 15 16 17 18 19 20

Olivia likes to draw.
She drew 7 pictures.

●●●●● = 7 = seven

1 2 3 4 5 6 7 8 9 10 11 12 13 14 15 16 17 18 19 20

There are 8 students.
They are playing a game.

1 2 3 4 5 6 7 **8** 9 10 11 12 13 14 15 16 17 18 19 20

Mia plays outside at recess.
She drew 9 **hopscotch** squares.

●●●●●
●●●● = 9 = nine

1 2 3 4 5 6 7 8 **9** 10 11 12 13 14 15 16 17 18 19 20

An **abacus** has beads. There are 10 rows of beads.

⬤⬤⬤⬤⬤
⬤⬤⬤⬤⬤ = 10 = ten

1 2 3 4 5 6 7 8 9 **10** 11 12 13 14 15 16 17 18 19 20

Gaby has 11 kids in her class.
They run a race.

1 2 3 4 5 6 7 8 9 10 **11** 12 13 14 15 16 17 18 19 20

There are 12 pencils.
The pencils are different colors.

●●●●● = 12 = twelve
●●●●●

1 2 3 4 5 6 7 8 9 10 11 **12** 13 14 15 16 17 18 19 20

Ms. Lee teaches art class. She has
13 **scissors** for her students.

●●●●
●●●●
●●●●
● = 13 = thirteen

1 2 3 4 5 6 7 8 9 10 11 12 **13** 14 15 16 17 18 19 20

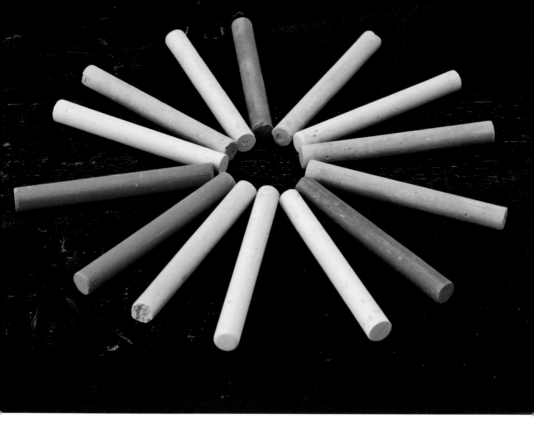

Chalk is used on a blackboard.
There are 14 pieces of chalk.

= 14 = fourteen

1 2 3 4 5 6 7 8 9 10 11 12 13 **14** 15 16 17 18 19 20

Mason likes drawing stars.
There are 15 stars on the chalkboard.

| ●●●●●
●●●●●
●●●●● | = | 15 | = | fifteen |

1 2 3 4 5 6 7 8 9 10 11 12 13 14 **15** 16 17 18 19 20

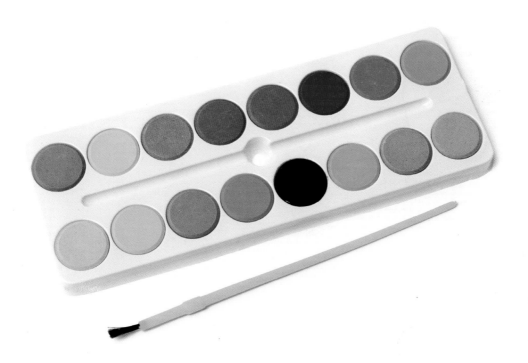

At school, kids use paint in art class.
There are 16 colors of paint.

= 16 = sixteen

1 2 3 4 5 6 7 8 9 10 11 12 13 14 15 **16** 17 18 19 20

There are 17 boxes. The boxes
are made from folded paper.

⠿ = 17 = seventeen

1 2 3 4 5 6 7 8 9 10 11 12 13 14 15 16 **17** 18 19 20

Kids have **lockers** at school.
There are 18 lockers.

● ● ● ● ●
● ● ● ● ●   =   18   =   eighteen
● ● ● ● ●
● ● ●

1 2 3 4 5 6 7 8 9 10 11 12 13 14 15 16 17 **18** 19 20

Crayons are used for coloring.
There are 19 crayons.

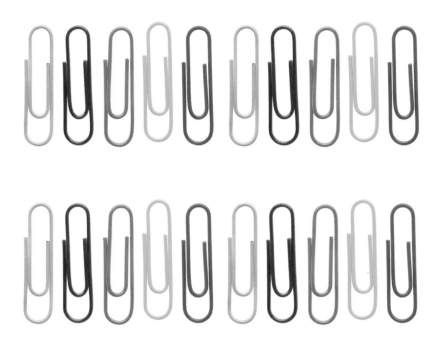

Paper clips hold papers together.
There are 20 paper clips.

twenty

1 2 3 4 5 6 7 8 9 10 11 12 13 14 15 16 17 18 19 **20**

Glossary

abacus – an instrument with beads that slide along rods that is used to do math.

chalk – a stick made of soft rock used to write on blackboards and sidewalks.

hopscotch – a game played by jumping on numbered squares.

locker – a closet with a lock that a student can put personal things in.

scissors – a sharp tool with two blades used for cutting.

violin – an instrument that makes music when you rub a bow across its strings.